Seeing More Than Clouds in
Your Coffee

Stories of a Psychic Medium in New York City

Catherine Nadal

authorHOUSE®

AuthorHouse™
1663 Liberty Drive
Bloomington, IN 47403
www.authorhouse.com
Phone: 1-800-839-8640

Some names of people and places mentioned in this book have been changed. Others, however, gave permission to use their names or are now deceased and living in the afterlife.

This book is a variety of short stories about coffee, psychic, and mediumship readings from my life of as a psychic medium. I have spent more than twenty years as a registered nurse and army soldier. This is a guide for those who seek to understand psychic abilities and for those who are interested in enhancing their own awareness. This book relates my experience in working with those who are skeptics, those who are believers, and those who are just curious about the afterlife. This is a reflection of working with the gift of spirit and the lives of those I have been able to assist.

The title of this book was inspired by the lyrics of the song "You're So Vain" by Carly Simon.

Published by AuthorHouse   11/27/2012

ISBN: 978-1-4772-7892-5 (sc)
ISBN: 978-1-4772-7891-8 (hc)
ISBN: 978-1-4772-7890-1 (e)

Library of Congress Control Number: 2012918735

This book is dedicated to those I have loved and lost and who are now living in the afterlife.

'Til we meet again . . .

CONTENTS

Kris Kancler
Super Star

FOREWORD

Having spent most of her career as a nurse and a military officer in the United States Army Reserve, you would think that Catherine would have had her fill of helping others during her professional journey. But this isn't the case.

I first became acquainted with Catherine through her show of support with the mission of the Rock Star Super Star Project. The words she shared were intriguing, and she conveyed a sense of confidence, leaving one with a feeling of security and comfort.

Catherine Nadal has a remarkable gift; she has the ability to sense things beyond the normal perspective, to see things unfold before they happen. Her psychic gift is something one doesn't experience often, and no one can deny her willingness to share this foresight in words that offer hope.

I have seen through my work with the Rock Star Super Star Project the benefit of sharing optimism and wisdom. Any type of work that involves supporting individuals in overcoming self-destructive behaviors, including addiction issues, isn't an easy task. Catherine's tireless work assists those still suffering, helping them to understand that in order to heal, self-love and strength must come from within.

I am grateful to have crossed paths with Catherine. Through her wisdom, I have become more enlightened about the importance of connecting the dots between parent and child regarding substance abuse. In addition, her influence in the world of pop culture and her relationships with those in the entertainment industry have helped further the positive impact of her own mission, bringing people together in extraordinary ways and allowing them to live a life of purpose and dignity.

As the reader of this book, your task is to uncover and document your own journey, just as Catherine has done within the pages of this book. You will find many tools to support you on your path to self-discovery while reading *Seeing More Than Clouds in Your Coffee.*

Thank you, Catherine, for your indefatigable and passionate dedication to extending a hand to others through your very insightful, inspiring, and encouraging words. You awaken hope and bring about healing.

Kris Kancler
Super Star
President/CEO, Rock Star Super Star Project (RSSS)
www.rockstarsuperstarproject.com

INTRODUCTION

My name is Catherine; and I am a professional psychic medium. This gift has been part of my life since my childhood. Many people are amazed by the work of a psychic, while others are skeptics, and still others are just, plain and simple, non-believers. I choose to embrace everyone and all points of view. I do not judge anyone based on a person's beliefs, nor do I expect that my life or beliefs should somehow be accepted by everyone.

I have always been sensitive to others and to future information, especially during difficult and challenging times. Dangerous situations have heightened my psychic ability and have tested my own beliefs. After serving in a combat zone, I decided to share my gift publicly with others.

Some people might see being a psychic as a curse, but I have never looked at it that way. I know in my heart that this is a gift from God. As with any gift, I have to protect and take care of it. I have chosen to treasure my gift. My life is different from most people's lives, as is my path in life, and I am grateful and honored.

Although I spent a childhood consumed by predictive dreams, I never planned a career as a psychic medium. I have worked in the field of nursing and received bachelor's and master's degrees. Early in my nursing career, I sought financial assistance for my education and joined the United States Army Reserve. The Reserve promised me a bachelor's degree in exchange for hard work and adventure. In May 1991, I couldn't raise my hand fast enough to join. It has been an amazing experience, serving with brave, intelligent, and caring men and women, both stateside and overseas. I have seen many states and countries that I never dreamed I would visit. Also, I have had the opportunity to experience different cultures and witness the brutal impact and effects of war. Through this work in combat, I drew in the true meaning of life, tossing out previous perceptions and disbeliefs. I realized that we sometimes find our true selves when going through the toughest challenge.

A psychic is psychic no matter where they go. I packed four duffle bags for my tour of duty but also brought my psychic ability.

It is important to understand that psychics can't predict their own future. They can get glimpses through dreams or visions, but helping themselves with this gift is not done easily. There have been many ups and downs in my life. Many people have asked me, because I am psychic, why I didn't see something coming or why something negative happened to me. Psychics are humans and need to learn many of the same life lessons as everyone else. My belief is that we need to experience all emotions, so that we can effectively help others sort out their emotions and ease them back on their path in life.

Sudden death is one of the most challenging aspects of my work. I have experienced many sudden deaths and have helped others at such times as a psychic medium. Death, no matter how it occurs, is a great loss to those who are left behind. I experienced my first sudden death at age sixteen, when my mother died. Many times, I have heard clients say, "I never had a chance to say good-bye." This statement always breaks my heart. For many people, death is final. That is one of the reasons that I share my gift of being a psychic medium. I am able to communicate with those who have crossed over.

The best sessions with a psychic medium are the ones filled with incredible evidence of the person who has died, with details of the life that person lived. Very often, the deceased person will communicate the mode of passing, his or her name, family members' names, favorite hobbies, and the work he or she did in life. These sessions are beautiful, loving, and at times, funny. Of course, the sessions do not bring the loved one back, but they do offer a sense of relief that the loved one is all right and that love never dies. I believe we will meet our loved ones again in the afterlife.

Seeing More Than Clouds in Your Coffee is a collection of stories of the psychic readings that I have given. The stories contain interesting details of readings using coffee, tarot cards, and mediumship. It's important to understand what you have endured in life in order to reflect and prepare yourself for what lies ahead. Psychic readings help detail your past, present, and future. On the pages that follow, I want to share my knowledge, experiences, and parts of my life with you.

CHAPTER 1

Symbols

Recently, I was sitting in a cozy restaurant in the heart of one of my favorite cities in the world, Madrid, Spain. I was with some friends and family I hadn't seen in a long time. After dinner, we each ordered a cup of coffee as we continued to catch up with one another's lives. Following my cousin's last sip of coffee, he leaned over and asked me to "read" his cup. For those who do not know me well, one might think that this is an odd request. However, as an avid coffee-cup reader for the past twenty years, I have read hundreds of coffee cups for close friends, family, and clients. This particular night in Madrid, we smiled over his cup, and as we were gazing over the images inside, other people in the restaurant began to stare at us. Of course, when I grabbed my camera from my bag and started taking pictures of the cup, we noticed more faces looking our way. I can totally understand their curiosity, but as I've always said, every good coffee symbol deserves to be photographed.

In one way or another, we all follow signs and symbols in our everyday lives. We encounter them daily, either consciously or unconsciously. We look for them to guide us in a specific direction. Signs and symbols give us meaning and represent important aspects of ourselves and the world around us. They often assist us in understanding life's fortunes and misfortunes.

From an early age, I knew I had a special gift. However, it soon became obvious that I had a lot of work ahead of me before this special gift could be fully realized and shared. I had to figure out what to do, and I needed to sort out my feelings about my gift. I decided to keep it to myself and just acknowledge my own sense of knowing through descriptions of my dreams or visions. At age nine, it first occurred to me that I knew something others did not. One day while fishing with my father, I knew when to pull up the crab net and instantly understood what my "intuition" had told me. That day, my father smiled from ear to ear as everyone gathered around to see the biggest crab caught in my net. As I stood there in silence with a feeling of satisfaction, deep down inside I knew how and why I'd caught that crab. I think that was the first time I was truly aware of my psychic abilities. Many years later, this gift developed so well that I was able to have accurate predictive dreams, see and communicate with the spirit world, read coffee cups, and work with honored tools such as tarot cards.

Reading coffee grounds and tea leaves is an ancient tradition known as tassology. Tassology is also known as tasseography. Over the centuries, tassology has been practiced throughout the world, very often in European and Middle Eastern countries. These days, this practice is fairly uncommon in the United States. Many people who ask me to do a coffee reading for them do so because they have previously experienced this in their culture and family. Many people are very superstitious about having this type of reading.

Tassology involves reading the images formed by the leaves or grounds in the cup after one has drunk from it. No one else in my family, to my knowledge, is a psychic, nor has anyone ever worked publicly in this field. I do believe my mother had a strong curiosity for psychic awareness, as I still have her 1950s-style fortune-telling wooden sticks and a personally signed copy of Jeanne Dixon's book on reincarnation.

Today, I often think of how I would have enjoyed having a conversation with her to find out her thoughts and possible hidden skills. However, she is now living in the afterlife, and we did not discuss my gift while she was alive. She did have a wonderful imagination and always comforted me after I'd had vivid dreams by telling me to focus on a field of pretty, colorful flowers. She loved gardening, nature, adventure, and life itself.

Not until 2005, when I returned from working in a combat zone as a soldier, did I realize I could no longer hide my psychic abilities. Within months of returning home, I questioned helping the public with my gift. Once I set the intention and asked for guidance, the universe answered, and I received many offers to work at psychic fairs.

One friend, Paula Caracappa, called and asked me to attend her psychic "Goddess Fair," with a special request for me to read Italian coffee. I attended the fair with my espresso machine, thinking I would be alone for most of the day and no one would be interested. To my surprise, however, many people were truly fascinated with the idea and the coffee readings. From that fair on, I continued to make connections for people through the coffee readings, and I have read at many fairs since. I have grown into my gift and started to provide readings by using tarot cards, playing cards, automatic writing, psychometry, and photograph readings.

Many symbols and signs are filled with color and are very often bright objects that get our attention and represent something symbolically to us. In life, we quickly learn how to identify them. For example, we learn a stop sign is a red-and-white octagon that gives a command to stop. We also understand that a traffic light uses three colors, each of which gives a different command to go, slow down, or stop. Signs also give us warnings of potential dangers, such as high voltage or potential for fire. "Ah, life should be so easy," we could say. If only we had life signs to help us when we meet a new problem. The signs could assist us in knowing whether to go, stop, or slow down. However, if we were given such warning signs to steer us clear and alert us of potential dangers or mishaps before we would encounter them, would we ever learn a lesson? Most likely not.

Compared to signs, symbols can be more complex and profound. They exist in many forms. Each symbol can represent different meanings for different people. For example, the symbol of the cross, for some, represents a community of faith. Another example of a cross is the Red Cross, which symbolizes medical care and in previous battles was commonly seen on the arm of a soldier providing medical treatment. Another example of a cross can be seen in various national flags, such as Switzerland, Finland, and Iceland, representing their pride, respect, and reverence.

Symbols can also generate great emotions in individuals. Symbols can change for people; the same symbol can cause different feelings many years later for people who have experienced a shift in their life. I have heard this from three people who had experienced losses at Ground Zero in New York City. It is known that after the smoke cleared and ashes settled, the cross at Ground Zero appeared. The cross, which was one of many thousands of I-beams that were originally used to construct the Twin Towers, appeared upright in the ground. Those at the site saw the cross in the midst of many other smaller crosses. At twenty feet tall, it stood in the middle of mounds of concrete, metal, and human remains. The workers at the site, both rescue personnel and firefighters, began to memorialize the cross by etching dedicated personal messages. This cross was lifted and placed at the corner of Church Street, as a symbol of liberty and freedom to everyone who passed it. There is an iconic picture that was taken at Ground Zero on September 11 that showed three New York City firefighters raising an American flag. The picture was shown in the newspaper the following day, and soon after, it appeared all around the world. In 2002, President George W. Bush unveiled a "Heroes 2001" postage stamp. This is another example of symbolism and how it is important to honor those who passed, to remember them and never forget. All of these symbols created a new meaning for these three people I met who had a significant loss at Ground Zero.

One person described the American flag that flew over the site as inspiring a "new feeling" of being a proud American and knowing the pain of being part of that day. Another person spoke of the cross and how real it made the situation feel to him and how his faith brought him through the experience. One woman shared with me that every time she sees firemen wearing their helmets, she is reminded of the fact her husband is gone forever. For those of us from New York City, this tragic event has changed life as we once knew it. Our skyline has changed; in our hearts, we knew something had happened that bright day that would be with us for a lifetime. As the smoke rose from our magnificent skyline, we knew that our world would never be the same again. That clear September day, we shed many tears, hearts were shattered, but somehow we were reminded of how strong we really are. Americans learned to stand together and face tomorrow in the midst of the unknown.

In the years following the attacks, I attended numerous 9/11 events, many of which were 5K races throughout New York City. Some of the events were fund-raisers, charity events, and dedications. I learned a lot about the lives of the men and women who perished that day. I found them mostly through the stories of their friends and families and reading their names and seeing their faces on the backs of T-shirts that other runners were wearing.

Their youth was documented in their dates of birth, which took my breath away. These T-shirts stopped my heart for an instant, and their smiles brought tears to my eyes. One runner had to stop, because the rubber on the sole of his sneaker fell off. He tied the sneakers together, hung them over his shoulder, and completed the race barefoot. We were running on the West Side Highway, which they had closed for the race. That image has stayed with me, and I know it will for a very long time. Symbolically, his sneakers could be seen as a protection or something essential or needed. Clearly, after this tragedy, it was apparent to many that his heart and mind were somewhere else. Perhaps what he needed he felt was no longer here. True love is precious, and some people never find it. But that day, I witnessed it, as I jogged behind the barefoot man with his lovely lady at his back.

A wedding ring is a symbol of a union between two people. For a happily married couple, it can remind the wearer of feelings of happiness and contentment. For a couple in a troubled marriage, a wedding ring symbolizes feelings of sadness, anger, and heartache. For those who have never married, the symbol could represent fear, disappointment, or freedom.

Understanding that symbols represent events in life is how I began to associate meaning to the symbols being shown in my coffee readings. Through my own life experiences, I have associated meanings to several symbols. As such, I am able to convey the messages for those I read.

As a child, I often had dreams that were predictive. These dreams were dramatic and often very scary and accurate. Some were disturbing, such as the passing of a life of someone I knew. When I was a child, after our family cat, Toy-Toy passed away, I remember seeing her in my dream. In the dream, I watched her running outside, looking healthy and happy again. Just prior to her passing, she did not move much, because she was sick and often hid under furniture. After waking from the dream, I knew in an instant that she was fine. I also believe that in the afterlife, we lose the aliments and illnesses that we carried in life.

As a child, I was never afraid of the dark; rather, I welcomed it. This often brought on debates between my sister and me about turning off the nightlight. The darkness was inviting for me, and I felt more relaxed, as if I was sleeping outside under the stars. Many years later, we had glow-in-the-dark stars pasted to the bedroom ceiling, and once this occurred, I really slept soundly. I knew I was connected to the stars and sky in my own personal way. I was in my element, and this was my introduction to a personal fascination with watching the moon and stars.

I have always loved nature and all it has to offer. As a young child, I often sat on my front step and watched the leaves move in the trees. I carefully watched as the branches and leaves formed different patterns and pictures each time the wind blew. One tree had branches that grew into a wonderful rabbit-ear shape and thick green leaves. Those rabbit-ear branches are still there today, even bigger and better than ever. I've always enjoyed watching the clouds that, on clear days, could tell stories all on their own by the images they formed. I know now that from a young age, I had a keen eye to see images in various objects.

In my teenage years, I was introduced to Francine, a psychic. I prefer not to call her a card reader, because she was more than that. She was truly gifted. I was about seventeen years old when I first went to her for a reading. At that time, I knew very little about psychics. During the reading, she immediately impressed me with her ability to tell me the details of my home, even down to the floor plan. This was my first encounter with clairvoyance. She also told me facts pertaining to people very close to me, including how my mother passed. I was not fearful, as I understood her abilities immediately and respected them.

A couple of years later, a friend introduced me to a woman from Armenia, whose name I have forgotten. She could read Turkish coffee. She could attach a message with a meaningful symbol or symbols that were created from the coffee stains left behind in the cup. I walked into her house for a reading, and everything seemed normal. However, by the time I was ready to leave her house, everything in my life had changed. I found that the coffee reading was the missing link to how I was able to see and hear with my gift.

She made Turkish coffee, which is thick, dark, and bitter. She filled the small cup and instructed me to drink it. When I was finished, she showed me the symbols in my cup. I immediately saw everything she saw. It was something that connected all my years of imagery together. When I told her I could read the cup, she smiled. I pointed out the images, and without hesitation, she said, "Oh, you can do this." After that experience, whenever I went out with friends, I gave them very accurate coffee readings. I was even surprising myself, as the information I gave seemed exceptionally realistic and meaningful for my friends.

CHAPTER 2

Coffee

Being psychic and giving readings has assisted me in being more open-minded and aware, especially since I receive many messages through my dreams. I use my own life experiences to make sense of what is being shown to me. I can then relay the messages to those I am reading for.

I cannot tell you how many times people ask me if they need to drink the coffee in order to have a reading. They explain various reasons why they cannot drink it. I then explain that they need to drink it for the reading. A few non-coffee drinkers will drink the coffee just to have the reading. It's quite comical to see people trying to swig it down. Some people close their eyes, slam their hand on the table, or even chase it down with a cocktail or beer.

Espresso, which is unique and much different from brewed coffee, is what I use for most of my readings. It is very bitter tasting. Even after adding sugar to it, some people still find it difficult to drink. I never limit the amount of sugar someone wants to add, as I can even read the sugar, if more remains than the coffee. A few people have asked me to read using Turkish coffee instead of espresso coffee. Turkish coffee is the style of preparing the coffee; it is not the actual type of bean or brand of coffee. Turkish coffee appears darker and richer and is a thicker beverage; it is much different from espresso coffee. Turkish coffee, like espresso, also can be made on the stovetop, but the final product is not similar. I believe people acquire a taste for their choice of coffee and tend to stay with their choice over their lifetime. Many of my clients choose Turkish because it is something they were raised drinking.

I often make the espresso in my kitchen, and I use a commercial machine, since it can be brewed quickly in this way. I use Italian espresso for the majority of my readings, since many people are familiar with it. Also, it is very common to find Italian espresso on the menu in many restaurants. The type of coffee used does not affect the outcome of the reading. No matter which type is used, the reading is always unique and interesting.

In preparation for any coffee reading, I always tell people, "If the cup is clean and no coffee remains, it means you do not have a message." In all my years of conducting readings, this has only happened once. Roseann, an old friend of mine, requested that I give her a reading. At the time, I was preparing to leave the country for a period of time. Roseann was familiar with my readings and wanted one before I left. I agreed, and we met at an Italian café in Queens. When I looked into the cup, it was perfectly clean.

Mine was not, but Roseann's clearly was. I said, "Sorry, there is no message." Roseann was surprised and disappointed, as she felt she needed some information and a solution to her present dilemma. She offered to buy another coffee, but I declined. The cup shows what you need to know, focus on, or be prepared for. I explained to her that timing in life means everything. Just because you are ready in life does not mean life is ready to show you what you need to see, learn, or live.

Timing is noted in many of my psychic readings. In all of the sessions, I have explained that some people have a reading that is focused on what has occurred in the past six months, some have just the future six months, but most have past, present, and future in their cups. On rare occasions, there are only a few details shown in the cup. One image may not reflect time, but it is there to symbolize something of great importance.

I remember this happening once when Barry and I sat in a Brooklyn café on a September day. The main image was of a marlin; the fish was clear and detailed against the wall of the cup. I looked into his eyes and said, "You have Florida in your cup, which sits next to a showgirl or stripper."

Barry laughed and said, "Which is it?"

I said, "The image is of a young girl who entertains the public and uses her body to do so."

He smiled and admitted the girl was Linda, his ex-girlfriend, who was a professional model. She was coming up from Florida to stand by him during an important legal matter. This message to him was simple but meant a lot. Barry explained that the reading gave him a sense of relief, since it reassured him that she was standing by him in his time of trouble, even though in the past he had not always stood by her.

Very often, symbols in the cup will show an event, person, or time from the past. During a reading at a psychic fair, I looked at my client, Helen, and smiled, telling her, "Your son is about seventeen years old. He has dark brown hair and loves to wear jeans." She looked at me confused. I continued, "He holds his hands deep in his pockets and is slouched down in this position." I stood up and illustrated how the boy stood by using the imagery in the cup as my guide. I held the position. Helen looked at me again, confused. "Well," I added, "he stands next to you and a house."

"Oh," she said, smiling, "that is my youngest son, Pete. He is helping me buy a new house. But he's not seventeen anymore; he is forty."

I then explained that many times in coffee readings, a person will be represented by the appearance they are known best, so that the reader can explain exactly who the person is. In this case, Helen had two sons, but when the boy was described to have had jeans on, looked about seventeen, and how he stood, she knew exactly which son it was. She was very happy about this image, since she was currently buying a new home, and it was a huge transition in her life.

Many times in life, we do not realize how people deal with themselves during a difficult situation. Sometimes during a coffee reading, the cup displays how we are handling the situation. Marie sat in front of me with her cup, very excited to hear her reading. I explained there was a large object in her cup, the likes of which I had never seen before. It was a robot with very large arms. It almost looked like a depiction of an action figure or superhero. I explained this represented a time when she had incredible strength but also was able to wear a type of "armor" that deflected all negativity. Marie's smile faded as she shared a memory of how during recent months, she had cared for someone who was chronically ill, while simultaneously dealing with the criticism of others. She was very grateful and thanked me numerous times for helping her to understand that difficult time in her life.

The past is often very important to people and often shows up in readings. Many times, I am able to see symbols that represent past events. Some include family members, while others focus on important personal events. I once sat with Sue for her second reading with me. Before this reading, she talked about the previous reading that I had done for her a year prior. She remembered me seeing an owl symbol in her cup. The owl was looking back at the past six months. I told her that she was living in the past too much and she needed to move on. Sue raved to others about that "owl" for the entire year until she saw me again. She explained to me that she realized she was looking in the past too much, as I told her. Sue admitted that having the reading and understanding what she was doing in her life gave her the wisdom she needed to change it. She decided to stop obsessing about the past. Sue quickly moved her thinking to the future, as she felt more prepared for it.

Most people admire love. Love at its best is romantic, passionate, and true. A wonderful universal symbol of love is a heart. I once saw a heart, tiny and floating like a jewelry charm, in Stephanie's cup. Stephanie was soon to get married. This symbol was significant, since as I explained to her, "You are giving your heart away with ease, like it's floating." She smiled and explained this was her second marriage, and she truly believed she was finally "in love." So it was with ease that she was "giving her heart to another."

People ask me if there was ever anything I saw that surprised me in a cup. In response to this, I tell them the story of a psychically gifted dear friend of mine named Louise Johnson. Louise had recently been released from the hospital after suffering a massive heart attack. She phoned me and asked me to bring my coffeemaker and coffee cups to her house. I repeatedly told Louise I did not think she needed that much caffeine, since she just had a heart attack and was on several new medications. Louise laughed and told me, "Just one cup." I arrived at her home and set everything up at her kitchen table.

As we sat at the table together, we were surrounded by statues and candles and enjoying the wonderful smell of her home cooking. To me, her house epitomized a home where the kitchen was the core, the complete center. Everything was done at the kitchen table: making pasta, serving eggplant-and-meatball sandwiches, paying bills, and even giving psychic readings. All events took place at that table for Louise. If her home were in a play, all of the scenes would take place at that table. So there I sat among the statues and burning candles and started to read her cup. I looked into her cup, and I jumped to my feet.

"What? What?" she asked anxiously while looking up at me.

I looked at Louise and said, "I can't believe it!" In the cup, within the past two-week time frame, was a depiction of her standing there with her left breast stretched out. The way I read coffee, I can depict time frames. This was her heart attack in the cup. I showed her the image, and she immediately let out a loud laugh.

Later, I asked Louise why she laughed, and she answered, "The doctor said it was a big heart attack." She always had a great laugh, a big heart, and a warm, wonderful sense of humor.

Louise was also a psychic reader, a very good one in fact. However, being human as we all are, she asked me a question: "If you did that cup reading a month ago, would you have been able to see the heart attack before it happened?"

I thought for a moment and replied, "No, perhaps not." To this day, many years later, my answer would still be no. Many times, symbols in the cup show us lessons and events, but it is very difficult in any reading to stop an event from truly happening, especially if it is destined to occur. Still, it is also important to remind others that we have free will. I very often use the example of sending out a résumé to apply for a job. If you do not send it, the employer will not know you are interested in the position. I once worked with a client who was very fearful of getting lung cancer but refused to stop smoking. I often reminded her that you do not have to be psychic to know that smoking two packs a day is dangerous. She often laughed it off, but deep inside she knew she had a true addiction to nicotine.

I believe that through readings, we can be better prepared for events or use the information to help us plan, handle, or cope, when the issue or concern arrives. I am a strong believer in everyone having free will. But I also believe in God. I believe that what is meant to be comes to be. One year later, Louise suddenly passed from an asthma attack. I will always remember that reading and will always cherish the friendship we had. Louise taught me a lot during our friendship. Most important, she taught me to believe in myself and to know that there are still good people in this world.

There is an old saying: "The truth is hard to hear." However, I believe that the truth is sometimes not so hard to hear; rather, it is something we desire and need to hear. A few years ago, around the holidays, I met up with an old college friend named Angelo at a local café for coffee. He agreed to have a reading. During the reading, his cell phone was ringing off the hook. As he took calls, I glanced in the cup, occasionally looking at him buried in conversation. As the last call ended, Angelo leaned in and asked, "What do you see?"

After staring at the symbols in the espresso cup, I said, "You have two loves." I added, "One is here, and one is far, but by spring, you will know your answer. However, your only problem is that you love them both."

Angelo smiled, thanked me, and then, in his usual casual manner, stood up, tossed money onto the table, and we left.

Many months later, I was sitting in an upstate New York airport, waiting for a plane, when my cell phone rang. I answered it, and there was Angelo's familiar voice, happily telling me about his summer wedding plans.

Sometimes people request readings near the place where they live. A friend's sister, Cindy, asked me to meet her in a café in Long Island, New York. Cindy had picked a particular café she liked. I distinctly remember it, since to me it looked almost like it was closed. It was empty except for the owner, who lingered in the back room. We sat in the café, and Cindy treated me to a delicious chocolate cake creation. While enjoying the cake, we drank the coffee in silence. She looked relaxed and seemed calm. However, her cup reflected a different picture. The cup revealed a series of dramatic changes, which were immediately happening to her. The most dramatic change was Cindy's newfound belief in her religion. There were many mountains that lined the cup, in a way that made them seem to be rising up. The symbol of a cross dangled very near the edge of one of the mountains.

As I described this image, she told me she had recently been experiencing problems in her life and had turned back to her religion for assistance. She seemed at ease with this message but was quite surprised how the symbolism matched her current situation. I explained that Cindy had climbed many mountains before, but she was still not finished with her struggles. She agreed, and although she acknowledged that she was still experiencing struggles, she felt a sense of relief. For Cindy, the reading justified why she presently felt an underlying feeling of excitement, exhaustion, and sadness.

A few years ago, I sat with an old friend's father, Tomaso, in one of his favorite Italian restaurants. We both ordered espresso, as we always do. We were conversing about the wonderful people we had recently met. I told him about the work I do occasionally at psychic fairs, in particular about the one at the Quest Bookshop in Manhattan. I explained that all of the proceeds at Quest were donated to back to help run the New York Theosophical Society. He often donated to charities and found this very exciting. He then humored me and agreed to have me read his cup.

Over the years, Tomaso has heard about people like me with this gift, but he had never agreed to have his cup read until that day. He had several things in his cup, but I focused on one clear image. I asked Tomaso if he had been around a dog in the last week or two, and he said that he had. I asked him if the dog was sick, and he told me it wasn't. I told him that the dog seemed to have a problem with its buttocks, because there was a marking of coffee on the image of the dog in that exact area. He then laughed out loud and said with a heavy Italian accent, "Yes, it's a male dog, but I saw him urinate like a female dog on my friend's front yard." Apparently, as I understand it, the dog had a recent surgery, during which a complication occurred that caused the dog to urinate in that way. I then asked about the significance of the dog's ears. Tomaso looked at me, puzzled. He could not figure it out.

I then said, "It seems like he hears for his owner, if that makes any sense."

He said, "It does!" He then proceeded to tell me that the dog's owner is partially deaf.

By doing these readings, I truly feel I am helping people. I believe that through these cup readings, I am assisting people in realizing things about themselves or about situations that might need some extra attention.

CHAPTER 3

Communication

For many years, I have worked as a communicator, formally and informally. Many people in my life are not surprised at the number of people I know. I have befriended people everywhere through my communication skills. I have kept many friends from past jobs, schools, vacations, and even exercise classes I've taken. I still keep the lines of communication open with several people I no longer see, including those who have passed on. The ease with which I am able to communicate with others is a great asset when I sit down with someone to conduct a coffee reading.

In my early twenties, while I was living and working in Manhattan, I enjoyed everything the city had to offer, especially the varied and exciting nightlife. I have many great New York City nightlife stories, but one of them in particular reminds me of a symbol I have kept in my mind all these years.

One night, I met a friend of a friend, who happened to be an expert skier, as well as a great-looking guy. He told me he wanted to show me his family. So we jumped in a cab and traveled over to Park Avenue. We got out of the cab and went up to a luxury apartment. Gazing at my watch, I knew it was late, but I had a feeling this trip was harmless and would hold some meaning for me. I was never so right! "The skier," as I call him, turned on a light in his apartment, which was decorated with expensive furniture and shiny hardwood floors. He walked over to a professional-looking photo of what appeared to be a family of professional skiers. This photo was mounted on his wall and looked like an advertisement. The skier then looked at me and sadly said that he never saw much of them but liked looking at the photo. It gave him a sense of being closer to his family. I felt his sadness, since his family was physically not close to him. To make up for that, he kept that picture close.

All of a sudden, he looked at the clock and said, "Make a wish quick; it's 3:33 a.m." So I did, and I silently wished for love and to have my own family one day. I still always make the same wish and have shared that "3:33 wish" with many people since then. The number three has become very powerful for me. The skier symbolized a loneliness that I never want, but by meeting him, I realized that someone so sad could remain hopeful for his future and for what he wanted most. He believed in the power of wishing on the number three, and to this day, so do I.

Does anyone really want to know the future? Some people say they do. A very good friend of mine, a fellow card reader, asked me to read her cup. She has been fascinated with this idea and with my talent for quite some time. She has even asked me to co-host guests in her home for coffee-reading parties. Believe it or not, even psychics occasionally need a psychic reading. I often joke with my friends that the psychic needs a psychic. I have had a few people, including my own doctors, jokingly ask me, "Why didn't you see this coming?"

We are humans, and we need to learn the same lessons and encounter similar emotions too, including pain, suffering, joy, and bliss. It has been noted that very often, psychics have unusually harder lives than most other people. Some people assume this is because psychics need to have experienced a variety of emotions in order to deal with others who may be suffering at different levels and periods in their life. Some psychics believe we need to know how it is to actually feel all emotions, through a variety of life events, in order to assist others, empathetically and compassionately.

Many times, people are quite amazed how a series of events coincides with a time frame that can be mapped out in a simple cup of coffee. During a coffee-cup reading with a client named Stacy, I explained two images in her cup that matched exactly with time frames in her life. One image of a rooster was paired up with a particular day in a month. I laughed and said, "This rooster is so clear; it's like it is saying 'cock-a-doodle-doo' in order to wake everyone up to something."

Stacy smiled and knew which event I was describing. She explained that it was when someone had voiced an opinion to a group of people, and my friend found out about it. This rooster event was followed by a whirlwind of changes for her, both socially and in her career. In her cup, there was also the image of a very small open parachute. It came after these changes in her life. I said to her that in the months ahead, she would finally be more aware of her surroundings. She would know what lay below her, and she would finally feel safe.

I have known a few paratroopers in my lifetime, and they all explain jumping as an amazing adventure, but when that chute opens, something internally makes them feel safe. That is how I connected the parachute in her cup to her life. Stacy totally recognized the importance of the chute in her cup and understood its meaning. Knowing the future is sometimes not as important as knowing how it will make us feel.

Just as in life, things during a reading are not always what they appear to be. A few years ago, I looked at Frankie's cup. Frankie has been a friend of a friend, and we have shared several friends together through our mutual circles. During Frankie's coffee reading I said that in the middle of the month of December, I saw a bobby hat, referencing the English police helmet. A look of total confusion crossed his face. I repeated the image numerous times and then clearly said that if it's not the hat, it's literally the name Bobby.

Frankie said, "Oh yeah, that is my friend Bobby." Through further explanation, the client explained that he'd had a serious discussion with this friend during this time frame, and the cup revealed the same. Images in the cup sometimes take on their own appearance to make a statement or send a clear message to the person.

Another example of strange symbols in coffee is animals. Once during a cup reading, an animal appeared, but it took on a strange appearance. The animal had the head of a pig and the tail of a beaver. This image was under the month of May, and it was shown with an image of the Virgin Mary statue lying above it. I literally described the animal in two parts to explain what I saw in the cup. In this case, I explained the symbol of the pig could represent the slang term for police officer, and the symbol of the beaver represented an animal that travels underground. I looked up at the client, who seemed annoyed and then, after rolling his eyes, stated he did not like the slang term, since he was a police officer. But then he smiled as he looked at me. I said, "Undercover cop?"

The man immediately smiled and said, "Yes, maybe." This man was a true skeptic and told me numerous times that he was not a believer. However, he said he sat for the reading because he was hoping to be promoted to the detective unit. He later explained the symbol of the Virgin Mary statue. He said his mother—who was named Mary—had been praying to the Virgin Mary for his promotion.

Certain symbols are universal, but some can take on different meanings for different people. It has happened that the same symbol has held different meanings in different readings. During one reading, I once saw the image of a very large spoon sitting in my client Melissa's cup. The spoon was under what appeared to be a block of time. Blocks of time are often explained by me as a "time frame." Time frames have a beginning and an ending. The spoon was very large. I laughed out loud, as you would have to have a vision impairment to miss it. I told Melissa, "During this time frame, you are spoon-feeding someone you would rather not be."

She smiled and said, "Yes, I was trying to avoid it for the longest time, but I can't."

I said, "The spoon is so large because it represents that the person really needs this from you. Your action is helpful."

The image of a spoon also appeared in another cup during a reading I conducted. I was sitting with a woman named Rita, and in her cup, I saw a pair of upside-down spoons under two different time frames. I explained this to her, and she looked a bit confused. I took the spoon she used to stir her coffee and turned it upside down. "Look," I said, "using the spoon this way is not helpful; it cannot hold anything." I then turned the spoon right side up, showed it to her, and said, "This way you can hold something in it."

She immediately understood. The representation of the upside-down spoons within two different time frames represented periods in the past six months when people were not helpful to her. Then I explained which months were assigned to the two time frames. She agreed that these were the times she received "no help." She verified all the information represented in the cup.

As a little girl, I remember being fascinated with seagulls. My family spent many summers at Jones Beach on Long Island, New York. The seagulls would fill the sky and rest on the boardwalks. They often landed a few feet away from me, hanging around for a while and then taking flight again. Birds have taken shape in many of my readings. Three birds in particular have made their appearance for significant reasons in several readings. During one reading, a woman by the name of Denise had a small bird presented in her cup, and I kept mentioning it as "tiny, tiny bird."

Denise smiled and said, "Yes!" The bird was sitting over the image of a bear. Denise went on went on to explain that because she was "tiny" as a child, she grew up with the nicknames "Tiny" and "Tweety Bird." She also added that she had been given a "bearlike" name when she joined an American Indian tribe. These symbols, while not meaningful to most, brought back significant memories for her.

In readings, the sizes of the birds vary, as well as their types and their colors. One evening, a few summers ago, I sat briefly in a café with a businessman who had traveled in from the Southwest. After I reviewed his cup, the only image that was represented was this glorious bird with large, outstretched wings. It was as if the bird was taking over the entire space inside the cup. I delivered the only message that this could mean: he would receive great news regarding a huge promotion. Months later, I received an e-mail from this man that very happily stated, "The cup was right!"

Most recently, I sat with a couple for a reading. George and Valerie were married for several years and were curious about having a reading. As George drank his coffee, a bird was forming in the cup right in front of our eyes. Valerie immediately saw it and revealed, "He has a bird in his cup." I let the couple know that often images that appear while drinking change or disappear once the coffee has dried. However, to my surprise, once the cup was lifted to be read, the image of the bird remained. I smiled and said, "Your bird stayed, but it has a firecracker on its back." I related the image of the bird to the image of the bird with the enormous wings I saw for the businessman from the Southwest. The message was the same. This bird image symbolized a work-related promotion, but the firecracker image represented that this action would cause a reaction in people. I told the man not to be too surprised if some people were not overjoyed by this promotion.

Most symbols have their own meaning; we just have to figure out what that meaning is. Very often an image appears in a cup that gives us a feeling of confusion, shock, or disbelief. I offer my interpretation of the image, and I wait for the acknowledgement. A recent example would be when I read for someone who frequently travels internationally. His name is Leon, and he is very active in many countries and handles many projects. Whenever Leon is in town, he takes a reading with me before leaving again. While he was back in town for a time, he could not resist the opportunity to squeeze a coffee reading into his busy schedule. Little did I know, his cup was already available. It seems he had taken the cup from a restaurant in New York City and kept it in his sport jacket, so that I could read it.

He pulled the cup out of his jacket, and I glanced down at it. One image immediately jumped out at me. I explained that there was the image of a tree that had been knocked over during a particular month. I explained the symbolism of a tree; it takes years to grow and is very strong. However, the one in his cup was knocked down. Leon immediately understood, and the image of the tree was quickly related to events in his life. He explained that over the past few months, he and his coworkers had had trouble with another employee. They were finally able to get the person fired for unprofessional behavior. He was in shock that they were able to get this accomplished but even more astonished that it was represented in the cup.

Communication is very important in life. My mother died suddenly when I was sixteen years old, and I realized that life is short. She graduated from Syracuse University and became an English teacher in 1954. She was very interested in communication. I learned from her how important it is to understand what someone is saying and, more important, not saying. I also learned that sometimes communication is not always verbal and that learning nonverbal communication can sometimes be very difficult. Very often, I will have someone record my readings or take notes, because sometimes we need to hear the communication again and again to confirm or to reaffirm the information.

CHAPTER 4

---◦◦◦)◧(◦◦◦---

Images, Meanings, and Messages

Each image represented in coffee readings has a certain meaning attached to it. I relate these meanings to the person who is having the reading. An example would be the image of the Statue of Liberty. As a child, I had family members who lived in Brooklyn, New York. My parents, sister, and I would often visit them. I remember being a small child, sitting on an old tire, while watching the tall ships sail in at the 1976 Fourth of July celebration. I also remember the drive there, which to this day is still my favorite part of driving in New York City. From the Gowanus Expressway—you can see the New York skyline and the Statue of Liberty perfectly. You also have a wonderful view of the old Brooklyn buildings and my family's parish, St. Michael's Roman Catholic Church.

The Statue of Liberty is a powerful symbol for New York and for the United States. The historic story behind the statue and the faces of many who began their new life at Ellis Island is profound.

For me, the Statue of Liberty is a symbol of freedom and clearly just that. My grandfather Joseph C. Nadal's name is etched on the American Immigration Wall of Honor at Ellis Island, as he is an immigrant from Spain; my nana's parents' names are listed, the Alonzos, as they emigrated from Italy. That wall makes me proud to see the many courageous hearts through the letters of their names. They, like me, loved the idea of an adventure, wanted a better life, and wanted to live in America. Who could blame them? After many years of living in New York, no other city impresses me more.

Over many years of reading coffee, I have only seen the Statue of Liberty in a coffee cup twice. The first time I saw it, I looked twice and blinked. It was beautiful and complete. I smiled at my client, Yvonne, and told her she was finally free of something, and she agreed. She added that she had recently divorced.

The second time the image of the Statue of Liberty appeared in a coffee reading, it was inside a tree. The tree was huge, with two branches that stretched over the top of the sitter's cup. The tree looked whole, but on closer inspection, the inside was shown to be rotting; it appeared empty and hollow. After a detailed evaluation of this image, I observed that the statue stood without her head. That symbol was dramatic. It represented "freedom without using your head." This individual was appearing whole to others but was self-destructing on the inside after finding a newfound freedom, which led her to careless living.

Animals are often a large part of people's lives, and the images of animals are often in coffee readings to represent behaviors or give warnings. Sometimes these images are there to represent something simpler: companionship. I was reviewing the past six months in a young man's cup. During this time, I explained that there was an image of a cat wearing a birthday hat. I said, "Wow, you were a happy cat."

Then he asked the month when this image appeared, and I repeated it. "Yes, I was a happy cat," he stated. He laughed and said, "That is when I finally got rid of my troubled girlfriend. I even threw a party."

Images of animals also often appear to give warnings. During one reading, a snake image appeared very clearly. This snake had spotted skin and a big cobra-like head with distinctive eyes. I explained that the snake was positioned during the springtime. I offered advice to Jan to be very aware of her surroundings and to be cautious of her belongings at this time. She was not frightened by this message but took it as a warning. Recently she shared with me that she had been told that she was acting very lackadaisically and carelessly by leaving her purse open with her private information exposed. The reading further stressed the importance that she needs to be more careful with her personal property.

At times, images of animals appear in coffee readings, and the message is easily understood. At one time, Wendy came into the psychic shop where I worked and asked for a coffee reading. She stood smiling while curiously looking at my table of colorful, decorated cups. In her reading, she had various images that I explained. I ended by saying, "You have an image of a huge dog in your cup." She immediately started to cry. She explained that her lovely companion, a favorite pet dog, had passed away last summer. She explained that she was so happy to know he is still with her, as she often feels his presence. The death of a loved one, either an animal or human, can take many years to accept, understand, and acknowledge. Through the cup reading, Wendy felt a comfort knowing her loving pet was still with her and protecting her in its own way.

Animals are companions, here and in the afterlife. I have had many mediumship readings myself where my father's dog, Lady, has appeared to the reader. Lady has come through to three different mediums. My father and sister were very close with her. I always considered Lady to be their dog, so I was a bit surprised to hear that she appeared for me. I believe she came through because it was through my friend Johnny that we met Lady. In the late 1980s, my friend Johnny wanted a new puppy. Once he heard the local animal hospital had a litter of new puppies, Johnny went down and picked his out. He returned home, smiling, only to find out that he was unable to keep the puppy, so he brought it to our house. We all felt sad for Johnny. When he returned it to the animal hospital, he told my dad and sister about the other puppies there. They went down and came home with Lady. Lady really was a surprise. No one in my family was talking about getting a pet, let alone something as specific as a dog. Johnny wanted a puppy but couldn't have one. As it turns out, my dad didn't want a dog, but he needed one since he was newly retired. Lady helped my dad during his retirement, and she helped him find out who his neighbors were after all his years of working. Very often, Lady started conversations by being an overly friendly dog who was lucky enough to find a special home.

The animals are waiting on the other side for us. I have witnessed many readings in which the unique pet names have come through or details about their pet-related illness. These pet readings are very touching, because the animals are very often cherished family members.

Frequently, only a partial image of an animal will appear. Recently, in my client Rick's cup, I saw an image of a man. In this image, the man was slouched over, holding his hands in front of him. A dramatic coffee stain sat where his hands were. The man was standing on elevated ground with a cliff positioned behind him. Across from this image was the front image of a heavyset frog. This frog was sitting and wearing a vest with three buttons down the front. The back of the frog was not visible, almost like it had disappeared. I explained this image to Rick. I told him that it represented a person who was the only one who could do something special with his hands on his job. Rick understood this imagery and agreed that this was true. I explained that the frog represented someone in a high position at his workplace. He was not sure who it was, as he has three bosses. Sometimes during a reading, it is hard to get the whole meaning. However, the awareness is important. Rick will evaluate things differently and be very aware of all of his bosses and their opinions.

This is a perfect example of how symbols represent situations that may not yet be clear to the person getting the reading. However, the information in the reading can help clarify future information as it unfolds. Rick now has confirmation that a man of high position was very much aware that he has this special talent. Many people, such as Rick, may not be aware of what really is getting noticed in the workplace and how they are valued. Some symbols have images that may not have any meaning for the reader, but to the person receiving the reading, it makes perfect sense.

I recently read a cup for a woman named Cecilia. The image showed her standing and looking stressed, with roses on the ground behind her. The roses looked like they would have if they'd been left behind on a gravesite. I said, "I would interpret that as letting us know that you have finally put something to rest."

She was very excited to hear this message and said, "Yes, I have finally decided to leave my apartment and stop fighting with my landlord." When I asked her how long she had lived there, she answered, "Nine years."

At times, I see images of families in cups. I explain each member by describing his or her physical appearance as shown in the cup or by describing the actions the image is carrying out. Sometimes the positions of the children are placed in an order to show who is literally closer to each other emotionally. There is a reading I can clearly recall, during which an image of a family appeared in a cup.

I conducted a reading for a young girl named Olga, who had emigrated from Russia. Her English-speaking skills were fair. I told her the image showed she was one of four people in her family. In the cup, the image showed her leaning with her head on her mother's shoulder. Her brother stood next to her father, while the coffee from her father's image leaked into the "heart" part of the cup. The heart of the cup is the bottom of the cup, or its center or core. I explained to her that she often cries on her mother's shoulder, but her dad is truly in her heart. Olga immediately understood this message, confirmed it, and began to cry. Her family was still in Russia, and she missed them dearly.

Just before the holidays, I sat with a woman named Monica for a reading. I explained that there was a family represented in her cup. This family had the marking of an overseas trip located over them, which meant they were from overseas or had traveled overseas during the month of September. Above the family's image were coffee markings of a pair of eyes looking down. I described the family as consisting of a mother, a father, and two children. In the description of the two children, I explained that one looked like an infant. After this, I related that I felt the children were grown, but one still acts like an infant. Monica confirmed the reading and explained that this was her sister's family. They came from Ireland during September to attend a wedding where everyone was very excited to see them. That's why there was the image of the eyes looking down at them. She also described her sister's boys, who were twenty-two and twenty-four years of age. She laughed and said, "The twenty-two-year-old always acts like a child."

During a reading with a young girl named Selina, I explained that she had one significant image in her cup. It was of a woman, wearing a gown with angel wing-like sleeves, who was raising up a child in her hand. The child was about five or six years old. I explained the child had short black hair. This young girl started to cry, as she recently came to the United States from South Africa. She explained that as a child, she had very short black hair and that her great-grandmother raised her from the age of five. Her grandmother was very proud of her, as she was the first member of her family to come to the United States. As she was getting up to leave, I told her she was very lucky. That image was a gift, and it was very beautiful. She couldn't wait to go to call her grandmother and tell her about the image.

A few months ago, an acquaintance of mine asked me to look at his cup. This person was aware of the readings that I do but was still very unsure and skeptical. I explained that there was a couple represented in his cup, a man and a woman, who were approximately the same height. I explained that the man seemed more stressed than the woman. There was an image of a child hiding behind the woman. He suggested that it was a woman he hoped to date who has a child. He did not want me to read further. Sometimes in life, people want to hear only as much as they feel they can handle. Again, life is about timing, and sometimes the coordination of events, places, and people helps us with the timing of situations and occurrences.

CHAPTER 5

Perceptions and Expectations

People often ask me what else I read. I find this question curious and reply with, "Almost anything." Over a casual conversation, I once read a man's hot chocolate. The reading was a surprise to him, and in the end, he remarked it was most accurate. That day, I actually surprised myself.

During a reading in a café, I glanced up at the wallpaper. The wallpaper had a blotted technique, and I used it as a teaching tool to explain to my clients how I see the images in the coffee. By doing this, I was able to prepare the coffee drinkers for the types of images the cup could reveal to them.

Many times during coffee readings, onlookers are fascinated and state that they never heard of such readings before. During the holiday season a few years ago, a friend of mine asked me for a reading. I met Eddie in a local café and read his cup. The owner, Irene, came over and asked me what I was doing. I told her about the type of reading, expecting her to be upset, as I never know how people will react.

Irene smiled and asked me to read her cup. After the reading, she dragged me into the kitchen, where she asked me to read for her sons, who were the café's chefs. They were all very impressed, and upon my leaving, they gave me a bag of holiday treats from the café as a way of saying thank you.

Sometimes, images appear "as is"; that is, how they are described. I once sat with someone who had never experienced any type of reading before. He had many images in the cup, but one was quite clear. It was described by me as "three lumps on a log"; two were sitting closely together, and one was further away. I explained that the log represented the common event or circumstance for three people. However, two of the people were more deeply involved. Eric listened intently, and at the end of the description, I asked if any of the information made sense. He stated, "More than you could imagine." He went on to explain that he had been involved in a legal action with two other people, and they were all awaiting trial. He added that he was recently notified that the other two were facing heavier charges and that he might be looked at separately in the case. At the culmination of the reading, I asked him how he felt it went. Eric explained that he was very satisfied with it because he was filled with anxiety, thinking about the future of the trial, but the cup reassured him of what he had been told.

In all of my readings, everyone receives the messages they are supposed to receive. I am not aware of the intimate details of the lives of those I read for. Therefore, people are often amazed at how their readings turn out. Many people have expectations prior to the readings, but in the end, they are generally satisfied with the messages they receive. Many times, the message touches a deep personal chord.

This happened when I met with a woman whose reading took a long time. Nancy had many images in her cup, but the last symbol was the most powerful to her. In the "heart" part of the cup, there was an image of a person that appeared to be encapsulated, as if in a bubble. I explained that it seemed like she had placed this person in a protective bubble within her heart. The woman became very emotional and broke down crying. There was nothing more I could say as I glanced at her, and then I asked if the message was okay. She perked up and said, "More than okay. I know of the person that you have described." She explained that she had made people feel trapped by her loving, maternal, doting personality. It literally drove away a lover of hers. Nancy admitted that she had visualized herself as more of a maternal figure toward him, rather than his lover. She felt the message helped her to come to the realization that she had to understand her future needs and wishes if she were to establish a healthy relationship with another man.

Occasionally, the coffee notes areas of concern. People are sometimes surprised by this, such as when I warn them about a potential injury or illness. During a reading, I explained to a woman named Rachel that there was a clear coffee marking in the area of her thyroid. I asked her numerous times if she had any medical problem concerning her thyroid. She mentioned that she had recent blood work performed, but the results showed nothing remarkable. About a week later, I received an e-mail from her, stating that the night after the reading, while lying in bed, she remembered that she has a polyp or growth in her throat. This is a good example of how very often people hear only the words, versus the message of the reading. I had stated "thyroid," when the message was "trouble in the neck/throat area." Rachel was unable, during the time of the reading, to make the connection of thyroid to the throat or neck until later on. During a reading, it is easy to get caught up on the words and miss the meaning. Very often, it isn't until later, after careful thought, that the message makes sense.

During the autumn, I ran into Karen, who I know really enjoys coffee readings. I had time to give her a reading, so we walked together to a local café. During the reading, I warned her of a weakness in or a potential injury to her left leg. I stood up and illustrated the location of the area of concern, which was indicated by the coffee. She insisted she had a problem with her right leg, not her left. I moved right along in her cup, since she had several other symbols to discuss. Before we parted from the café, I reminded her to be cautious regarding what I saw concerning her left leg. A few weeks later, I phoned her to relay a message for a friend. As we were ending our conversation, Karen gasped and said, "I forgot to tell you!" She shared with me a story of how she recently fell while in her kitchen, and she injured her left leg. She then humorously added, "I can laugh now, but at the time, it was very painful. When it happened, I immediately thought of you."

During another reading, I spoke with a man named Jack, and I told him he had recently been under a great deal of stress that affected his stomach. He immediately understood this message and agreed by replying, "You're telling me!" I then gave him several dates that occurred during the middle of the previous month. I stated that the fifteenth, sixteenth, and seventeenth were days when he had trouble walking. He experienced pain or something wrong with his feet. "No," he quickly replied, "I injured my back."

I asked, "Did you have pain when you would walk?"

"Yes," he replied.

This is another good example of how people hear the words, rather than the message during the reading. The message is always clear, but at times, the words or the sitter's thoughts get in the way.

Many people have stress in their lives from numerous sources. In the cup, I can see the stress represented, as well as how it clearly affects people. I can see timeframes indicated when these stressful events occurred. When I give a certain timeframe to people, they often instantly appear confused. During the reading, I ask people to remember the past. When I do this, people usually become concerned. They frequently say funny statements such as, "I can't even remember yesterday." Some say they can't remember last year or the year before. Many times, people are surprised at what they can remember when they actually try. They are also shocked at how quickly time flies when they realize dates and connect them with life events. When I describe a time frame during the past six months, people can't imagine how much has happened in their lives since then.

CHAPTER 6

Time

Throughout my life, I have been consciously aware of time. Time is an interesting thing to watch and track. As a runner, I wear a watch that tracks my calories burned, my heartbeats, and my running time. It does not track the actual time. Over the years, I have learned how many songs it takes for me to return home after a long run. While waiting for big events to occur, it is sometimes easier for me to count full moons rather than months. People often ask how long a coffee reading takes. My answer is always the same: "It depends." Literally, it takes several minutes for someone to drink the coffee and then approximately three to five minutes for the coffee to dry. The timing from there depends on the symbols, the messages, and the person who is receiving the reading. I describe the meanings of the symbols, some of which are more complex than others. I don't know how long it will take the sitter to associate with or understand the message and its meaning. The range of time it has taken to perform a full coffee reading has gone from five minutes to one hour.

An image will often appear during a time frame to represent how the sitter was physically feeling at that time. This was clearly seen in a coffee reading of a woman. An illustrated time frame revealed the month of September. During this period of time stood the image of a strong man who looked very athletic. On closer examination, he looked as if he were wearing high heels. The high heels represented that the image was of a very tall man. The image was turned and looking back, as if the man was reviewing the past. Two months ahead of where the figure of the athletic man stood was a stick-figure man, looking toward the past as well. Upon closer examination, the setting sun was represented by the coffee's spotted appearance. It was located behind both figures and was very distinctive. The setting sun was very symbolic in this cup reading, since the man represented in the reading was healthy and then had suddenly become ill. In the cup, the healthy-looking figure turned into the stick figure. It was a validation of what was happening to her loved one during a painful, stressful, and sudden illness. I explained that because the sun sets at the end of the day, the sun, therefore, represented an "end." In this reading, the setting sun represents completion; specifically, her family member was reaching the end of an illness. I let the sitter know that things would turn out okay for this man. I intuitively felt this.

The woman was still very concerned but also amazed at how the coffee captured the man's changing condition and actual appearance. She explained that his illness occurred very quickly, and the coffee depicted this. The woman noted that the figures were reviewing the past, since the man had experienced a painful summer filled with a new onset of arthritis. It was during the month of September that he finally felt strong again. Two months later, she revealed, he was suddenly ill, requiring hospitalization and multiple surgeries. After the reading, she felt a sense of relief and hope, seeing the image of the setting sun and knowing his illness would soon end.

Believe it or not, even movement can be illustrated in a person's cup. One month later, the woman from the previous reading sat with me for a second reading. The image of the same man had returned; however, in this reading, his image was airborne. It looked as if he was jumping for joy and spinning. The coffee around his figure was wispy, almost as if there was a protective cloud surrounding him. As I explained this to her, the woman was smiling. This man's condition had improved, and he was ambulating independently again. This woman clearly understood the protective cloud image. She explained that she had been present, along with a nurse, during an episode where this man almost fell. With the way this man's body was positioned at the time, both women could not believe how he remained standing. She believed it was the "protective cloud" that surrounded him, keeping him "airborne."

One day, while I was working a psychic fair, a lovely woman sat with me for a coffee reading. The clear images of a bride and groom took shape in her cup. The images stood together, dressed in wedding attire. The image of this couple was so clear and easy to see that the woman saw the image herself, without me having to point it out. However, in readings, things are not always as they seem. This reading proved that. For this woman, the images did not represent a bridal couple. The image of the groom represented the woman, and the image of the bride represented this woman's job. As I described the time frame and the concept of the new commitment with her career, she clearly and quickly understood the symbolism. She was just starting a new, higher-level position at her place of employment. I also let her know that the groom image had markings to indicate areas of concern pertaining to her health. I pointed these areas out to her. She verified all of them, as I described problems in the thyroid, abdominal, and lower-back areas. During the past six months, she had suffered from numerous ailments in all of these areas, and they have all stemmed from job-related stress.

Very often in life, we do things on a daily basis, and these events become an ordinary part of our day. However, the things we do can have a profound effect on many people. Often, we do not notice how important we are to others. During a reading with a woman, the image of a huge and beautiful angel appeared from the bottom of her cup to the top. This angel was dressed in white, and the coffee puffed out away from the cup. I was amazed and very excited as I described this image. I said that she must have done the work of an angel about three months earlier. The woman denied it and kept mentioning that she was confused about this reference. However, the image of the angel was so clear and beautiful that I persisted. All of a sudden, after careful thought, the woman mentioned that she worked in the medical profession. She had recently assisted in lifesaving measures on one of her pediatric patients. To her, this was just a normal part of her day-to-day routine. The cup wanted her to realize the good she does in life and how her life impacts others.

Sometimes images appear to justify how we are feeling. I read the cup of a woman who, at the time, was caring for two family members who were ill. One was sicker than the other, but both required much of her time and energy. In her cup was her own image, elegant, light, and ballerina-like. The image was bending over backward in a yoga-like pose. When I delivered the message that she was overextending herself and bending over backward, she nodded and agreed. She understood this description fully, and it greatly related to her life. She had performed ballet exercises in the past and was now working hard caring for these two ill family members. This message was clearly a description she could relate to, but it was also a confirmation of her activity and efforts. I also explained that during a particular month, she would be bending over. She understood, since the next four to eight weeks, caring for these family members could prove to be very stressful for her.

CHAPTER 7

Clairvoyance

I recently read for an elderly man who was curious about the concept of psychic readings. During the reading, I explained that there was a capital T in his cup and that I was getting the name Tom associated with it. I explained that Tom was married and was ill. I also described that his wife was at his bedside. The elderly man agreed and stated that Tom was a good friend of his. This man was very open to the reading and wanted to understand more, such as how I get information without using the cup. I explained to this man that being clairvoyant is interesting. In addition to using the cup to relay messages, I can see images in my mind that also enable me to describe and pass on information.

I was recently asked to visit someone who wanted a tarot card reading prior to major surgery. When I met with Dave, he was in his early seventies. I told him I saw a surgery in my mind. Upon discussion, Dave was insisting that the doctor mentioned only making small, hole-like insertions. I encouraged him to research more about this surgery, since I was getting that it would be more extensive than what the medical professionals were describing to him. During the tarot card reading, one card fell to the floor, a card illustrating "victory" or "success." Dave listened to the whole session but seemed to focus mostly on the card that fell out of the pile, since the message it held was very positive.

Many times, the importance in the reading lies with what the person walks away with. The positive message gave this man an easy feeling about his upcoming surgery. A few days later, I received word that the planned surgery would be more extensive than the man was previously told; it would require more of a surgical approach. Dave was not bothered or unnerved by this new information. Hearing this information beforehand prepared him and made him less nervous.

Since childhood, I have been aware that I am clairvoyant, clairsentient, and clairaudient. These gifts involve being able to see clearly and feel and hear clearly. I have several friends and associates who are mediums and are all very gifted, and their work is well documented. However, in the beginning, I never formally thought of myself as being a medium. I received a call from a friend who stated that her sister needed to speak with me regarding her mother-in-law. When I called my friend's sister, I realized the woman wanted me to communicate with her mother-in-law, who had passed on; however, she was asking me to see if I could pick up any information regarding her.

That night on the phone, I explained that I was not sure what I could get and had not done much work as a medium. I considered myself "new" at the time. I began by describing several items the woman had owned, the layout of her apartment, as well as habits she was known to have. I then described the place she had worked some forty years earlier. During the conversation, I was able to bring through detailed information about her mother, personal information only those close to her would know. My friend's sister immediately felt I had made a true connection with her family member. She said she felt relieved and ecstatic after the reading, as this verified for her that her mother-in-law was well on the other side and that death is not the end. But she also said the reading gave her some insight to the afterlife and decreased her personal fears.

This reading was truly a gift for the woman as well as for me. Since then, I have attended several formal training sessions, most notably the Arthur Findlay College for Psychic Mediums in Stansted, England. For those of you who believe in the afterlife, value any messages you receive from your loved ones who have passed on. These experiences can rekindle fond memories and provide peace of mind. They can give us the hope that comes from believing we will reunite with a loved one who has passed on. Since that first time, I have delivered some very inspiring messages to those who are interested in the gifts of a medium. The longer I work with spirit, the more amazed I am at how hard our loved ones work to get a message through to us. It is clearly evident to me that we don't really die; we just move on.

Me on Valentine's Day giving Tarot and coffee readings in
Fiamor Boutique in Dobbs Ferry, NY

Espresso coffee and oranges in Valencia, Spain (November 2011)

Coffee Cup Reading—To the far left there is a small image of person having a victory—their hands are literally up in celebration, the image in the middle was a reflection of the person I was reading, the figure has their head in the clouds over an issue, they choose not to deal with, as many other figures are standing around observing, this person is ignoring the issue

Coffee Cup Reading—Leprechaun as seen in a coffee reading I did for a client in London, the leprechaun represented many new changes in the person's ability to see their own talent and how lucky they truly are about a particular gift, the image "faces the future and it is sitting" which reflects the changes are just about to happen. Within two weeks time—the cup reading reflected the person's recent evalautation, where they received very high praise from supervisors in their work environment.

Coffee Cup Reading—This is one of the best photographs I have taken while using Turkish coffee. It shows very clearly the image of a woman standing in the middle of the cup, above her are images of people swirling around her. Two people stand out—a woman and a child. In the reading it was explained the grandmother was center or "heart" of the family and was keeping a close watch on her daughter and grandson. Who I said was having trouble seeing something clearly. Within days of this reading the person heard the grandson was prescribed reading glasses.

Coffee—slightly to the right at almost the 1 o'clock position is the image of someone with their arms stretched out and their head bowed . . . the color of the coffee has created a spotted appearance . . . which was explained that someone has been stretched and stressed beyond normal means over an issue which feels like a "self sacrifice" . . . the person agreed and said they had been worried over a family member and the person's declining health issues and was not focusing on her own health needs.

Myself, Rob Caggiano (Anthrax, The Damned Things) and my cousin
Matt DelRossi (singer/guitarist Nashville, TN) West Village, NYC

Cliff McLarnon on left, Glenn McLarnon on right (RIP)
(Band—Nervous Wreck)

The Chance Theater

Frank Pallett and Carolyn Pallett Brophy, owners of The Chance Theater

Deceased Dedication Tattoo submitted by Bob Cormican . . .
"This tattoo is in memory of my beloved wife who was my one true love,
very best friend, and now my angel. It serves as a daily reminder to
live through her virtues of unconditional love, positive outlook,
never-ending courage, and perseverance."

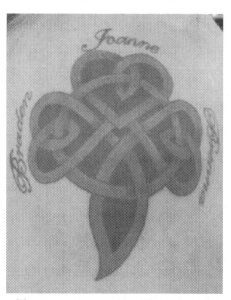

Living Dedication Tattoo—submitted by Major Jay Main—United States
Army- dedication tattoo to his living wife and children

Deceased Dedication Tattoo—submitted by Cliff McLarnon in
memory of his brother Glenn McLarnon.

Tarot cards-past present and the future—Dobbs Ferry, NY

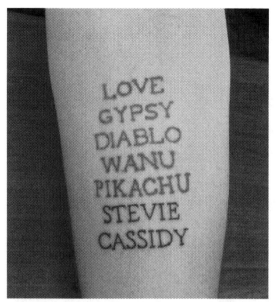

This tattoo is submitted by my friend Simone Reyes (Reality Star / Animal Rights Activist) it shows her undying love and dedication to her companion animals now living in the afterlife and to all animals big and small.

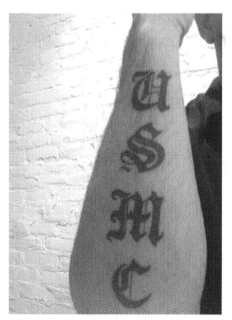

SGT Andrew DelRossi, US Marines
1st Bn 25 Marines B Co "USMC"

Me at Wave Hill on a Sunday in the summer—
this is one of my favorite places . . . such amazing views of the
Hudson River . . . Riverdale—Bronx, NY

CHAPTER 8

Dreams and Visions

As a little girl, I would frequently experience dreams and not know why I had them. I would sometimes be very concerned about the details of the dream. I remember my mother coming into my room to comfort me. She would tell me stories using her imagination and insight. Then she would tell me to close my eyes to relax. Soon after, I would fall back asleep and sleep soundly the rest of the night. My mother could not have been more comforting. Using that imagery with a small, scared child was the best thing she could have done. I will always remember and cherish those nights, as well as the beautiful places I envisioned.

Many years later, as I approached my late thirties, I attended a few hypnosis sessions, each conducted by a different practitioner. All of these experiences were different. I often tell a funny story about sitting on a sofa in a residence in Westchester County. I went to this session in an effort to quit smoking. The hypnotherapist was lovely, and I remember her telling me to count backward and stare at the bookcase in front of me. I woke up feeling like I was transcended somewhere for an unknown period of time. Time just flew while I was in the session, and I jokingly wondered if the practitioner went to do her laundry. Her black cat stayed by my side for the entire session, but the cat was not informing me; perhaps she too was hypnotized. However, I did stop smoking. I smile as I write this, still unsure if not purchasing cigarettes anymore was a conscious or subconscious decision.

One session in particular stood out from the rest of all of my hypnosis sessions. I lay down on the practitioner's sofa in his Midtown Manhattan office for a hypnosis session for a past-life regression. This was supposed to be part of a series of sessions to review my life and perhaps even previous lives. Under hypnosis, I recall trying very hard to remember, and in only one session, I actually let go and allowed myself to see something. What I saw was a beautiful field of wheat, golden and swaying back and forth in the warm breeze. The wheat was so inviting, so full of comfort, that I wanted to run toward it. The practitioner then called me back. I awoke calm and refreshed. If that is what we see when it is time to pass, I would be ready, and I would joyfully and peacefully keep going toward it.

I have had several visits from family members who have passed. These visits have been felt, not seen. I have often felt them caress my hair while I am driving. It feels so real when it occurs that the top of my head tingles for a while afterward. It is an amazing feeling. During these experiences, I usually call out, "I know you are here," or "Thank you, I needed that." It is a very loving feeling.

However, a few occurrences took a while to sort out or get used to, even for someone like me. I travel very often, for work and for pleasure. One summer day, after a long day of meetings, I returned to my hotel room. It was late in the day, so I prepared for bed and crawled under the blankets. The television was on low, and I was surrounded by these great big white pillows. Out of the corner of my eye, and out of the blue, I saw the clothes that I had laid out on the closet shelf go flying off and onto the floor. I leaped up and said, "Okay, I know you are here."

Walking around the room, I had the sense I was not alone but felt a familiar, comfortable feeling. I immediately looked at the calendar and realized the date of a close friend's passing was approaching. I smiled and remembered him and how he always liked to make me laugh. Perhaps this was his spirit letting me know I wasn't alone and that I needed to smile again and not always be so serious.

Once, as I was lying on the bed in another hotel room, I felt like a cat had jumped onto the bed and climbed across me. This was strange, as it was just about two months since my father's cat, Felix, passed away. Felix had recently been hit by a car in the middle of the night. He made his way home to pass away in the yard of my father's neighbor. Dad and I cried while burying him, which literally took hours, since neither my father nor I wanted to say good-bye. I know that Felix came to thank me, because I was the one who helped wrap him in a colorful Harley-Davidson beach towel and dug his grave in my father's backyard.

When I moved into my apartment in 2006, changes began to happen almost immediately. Coincidentally, this apartment had been my parents' first apartment in 1966, when they were just newlyweds. I truly believe that, from the afterlife, my mother sent me the opportunity to purchase it. Once I moved in, I realized the place needed a lot of renovation. As I began planning, I felt helpless, wondering how to speak with contractors and freelancers and stay within my budget. I asked my mother to help supervise this project, and numerous things suddenly came my way. One contractor told me about a man who could refinish my floors at a very low rate. To accept this offer, I had to move outside of my comfort zone and learn to trust complete strangers. I had to go through a series of similar experiences, as I quickly found out that I could have my dreams come true in an area that was very foreign to me. Trusting workers was a challenge for me. I have no experience or knowledge with construction, and I did not feel very confident. I reviewed all the people I knew and felt I had very little experience in renovations and almost no knowledge in design. I often felt frustrated and unnerved, especially since I wanted to create rooms with a unique European feel and style.

I decided to rely on those who have passed on and see what they would show me in my dreams. Sometimes I dream of someone I know, and the events in the dream will play out in the near future. The details of the dream may reflect anxiety, health issues, or sometimes just indicate that I will receive a call from them. Sometimes the dreams I have are detailed and involve people I've not yet met.

During my apartment experience, I paid complete attention to the details of my dreams and almost as much attention to the people I met who I wanted to work on the apartment. I looked at their names and addresses and even worked out dates on the calendar using numerology. I was very lucky, since many of the contractors I worked with gave me a unique style and feel in my apartment, which I can actually now call "home."

Many times, I am unsure of what a dream will show me. Here is a good example of a dream that, even over the years, I have not been able to forget. Once in the mid 1990s, I had a dream of a little girl about eight years old, beautifully dressed and with a cheerful smile. In the dream, she was holding my hand. It seemed like we knew each other very well, but we never spoke. We just walked around, somehow knowing where we were headed. A few months after having this dream, I was invited to a party in Westchester County. My connection to this party was my friend's cousin, who was getting married. At the party, her cousin introduced me to her fiancé's daughter, Merissa. There she was, the little girl from my dream. Upon my saying hello, she ran up to me and hugged my waist.

Everyone stood back and said, "She is very friendly," but I knew why she had done this. She looked up at me and said, "Hi." She then took me by the hand and brought me to the garden. I felt like we knew each other already. There were several functions at which I was in the company of these people. Every time I met Merissa, she had the same warm approach and smile. She would take me by the hand and lead me where she wanted me to go.

Some people believe in past lives, where people have experienced each other before. I believe in this connection. I have always believed this, and this girl was true evidence for me. I have shared this experience widely, since for many people, this is a new concept.

In the early 1990s, I dated a young man who lived with his mother. Instantly after his mother and I met, we created a strong bond. Very often, he would pace in and out of the room, waiting for us to finish speaking. He would joke with me, asking questions like when we should leave or where we should go, to prompt us to finish up. She told me wonderful stories about him as a child and explored my ideas on topics of interest such as politics, art, and literature. During this time, I was fairly new to the military and was focusing on completing my bachelor's degree. She often encouraged me to plan my future and dream big.

I recently heard from her son, who informed me that she passed away two years ago. My heart felt a pang of loss for this great lady. A special memory of her smiling, with a glimmer in her eye, crossed my mind. I felt lucky to have met her and made a bond with someone who was so creative, funny, and knowledgeable, at a time when I truly needed a friend and a mother.

I love traveling, especially taking trips overseas, and very often I travel alone. One trip I took alone was in 2008 to Madrid, Spain. Just recently, I returned from another trip to Madrid, and I know why I fell in love with it from the beginning. From the moment I exited the cab in downtown Madrid in 2008, I knew without fail which streets to turn onto to bring me closer to my destination. It was as if I had been there before, although in this life I never was. People across the street would wave at me and smile as if they knew me.

One day while I was there, I decided to attend a bullfight. It was a Sunday, and I knew it would be important for me. My grandfather was born in Spain, and I thought I really needed to experience the culture and traditions firsthand. Sitting and waiting for the fight to begin, I started to speak with a tourist from South Korea. He told me he was going home to enter the military, as he had not passed his exams to become a medical doctor. He seemed very disappointed and was using this time to explore his thoughts by traveling through Europe for most of the summer. I told him that I was a nurse and had been in the United States Military for many years; he looked shocked. He looked around, pointed to hundreds of people who sat waiting for the fight to start, and said, "Of all here, I sit next to you."

I assured him that he could join the military, and he would be surprised at how much it could teach him. In the short conversation, I saw the worry and fear escape his face and a smile wash over mine. For the rest of the bullfight, we compared our cameras and photos and cheered the fighters on, per traditional Spanish custom. A few months after that trip, I reviewed photos taken while I was there and realized something surprising: I could still see the streets and the directions in my mind. I thought perhaps I knew this Korean man before, in another life.

Sometimes in life, you realize something new. Recently, I took the train to Valencia, Spain, near where my grandfather came from. Apparently, I have many of the features of people from this area, and many people were approaching me and conversing with me. I found this very interesting, since I am the only one in the family who has these facial features. Sometimes in life, even when you feel like you do not belong, life places you somewhere for a purpose and gives you the feeling of belonging. That experience filled me with sense of gratitude that wiped away any sense of loneliness.

CHAPTER 9

Surprises—Even for Me

Not too long ago, I thought about surprises—how some of them are really good while others aren't. Still, they are what they are. I have had my share of them over the years. A memory of a good surprise in my life was when I was awarded a humanitarian award in nursing school. When it was announced at graduation, I had no idea I was even being considered. Some surprises come in disguise, meaning we are not sure if the surprise will present itself positively or negatively. Sometimes it takes time to figure it out.

Sudden death is often a surprise. Even the death of a loved one who has spent months struggling in medical treatment sometimes feels like a surprise to those left behind. Even if we try to fully prepare ourselves for the death of a loved one, it can come as a terrible surprise. I have experienced the sudden death of a family member, stranger, friend, and patient. All of these deaths were memorable, and no two were the same.

Last year, I was sitting at my kitchen table, reading the edits of this book, and I stood up to make the morning coffee. As I was standing in the kitchen, my best friend's mother's spirit seemed to be standing right next to me. She had passed a couple of years earlier, and I had assisted my friend in caring for her as she was dying. We called her "Maga," a name her grandson made up when he had trouble saying "Grandma." She was amazing. She had a smile and a sense of warmth that can only be compared to an angel. Maga was gentle, loving, generous, and forgiving. She is missed by many, especially her children. As I stood at the coffeemaker, I could feel her to my left, and within the minute that elapsed, I felt her warmth and sensed her thanking me for making the coffee. I thought, *I never made her coffee. She must be thanking Cookie, her daughter.* I turned around and saw this book, which Cookie was helping me to review. I then said out loud, "Oh, you know she is helping me with the book."

I sent off a quick e-mail explaining this event to Cookie. She e-mailed me back and explained that just the day before, she was in the Dunkin' Donuts by her house. She used to bring Maga to that same Dunkin' Donuts all the time after a morning of shopping. They would sit and have their afternoon coffee. That day, Cookie saw a woman paying for her and her mother's coffee, just like she used to do. As the woman looked back at her mother, who was sitting at a table, Cookie felt the loss of her mom.

When Cookie returned home, she spoke out loud to Maga. She told her she missed going shopping with her and then going to Dunkin' Donuts for coffee. She asked for a sign from her, to let Cookie know she is okay and that she is still around. Cookie opened her e-mail the following morning and read my e-mail about the coffee. The reference to her mother and the message from her, she felt was remarkable. She called me to thank me for relaying the sign she had asked Maga for. She said, "Now I know she is still with me, and everything is okay."

I was recently sitting with someone who suddenly started to talk about her child, who had passed many years ago. During the conversation, it was apparent that she was still grieving for this child, and she was not able to let go. This person walked me through the diagnosis, illness, and death. After working for many years in oncology nursing, I understand the effects cancer has on the patients and their families. There are many stages of grief, and sometimes people can get stuck in a stage. What is important in life is not to judge; no one knows someone else's pain, anger, or love. Only that person does. What is important is to acknowledge the person's love and dedication.

What I have learned through my work as a medium is that love never dies and that our friends and our family members do not leave us. They try very hard to let us know they are still with us. It often comes out in the simplest ways and very often in readings. For instance, I recently sat with someone and gave her a reference of a flower and a brick wall. I described the flower in detail, as I do not know the names of many flowers. I described it as delicate, with a wilted feel. I explained that it climbed up this brick wall of the house. The woman's eyes widened, and she explained that her mother had these wondrous morning glory flowers that grew up the outside wall of their brick house. Those flowers were her mother's pride and joy. This reference might seem simple and unimportant to some, but it is not up to the rest of us to judge what this reference meant to someone like her. This message meant the world to her, since it was a true connection to her mother.

I remember being surprised as a young nurse when I witnessed someone having a sudden heart attack right in front of me in mid-speech. I sprang into action, realizing what was happening, and I began to do all the things I was trained to do. The person survived, and I will always remember that moment when, as a young nurse, time seemed to stand still. When life takes an unexpected turn for the worse, either for ourselves or others, it can show us how short life is or how we need to start living life. After serving in Iraq, I realize how short and hard life can be but how truly wonderful it is. Most importantly, I learned not to take anything for granted.

CHAPTER 10

Just Ink, Music, and Symbols in Tattoos

Stepping into the already dark bar felt strange on a sunny Saturday afternoon. I was asked to participate in a Tattoo Expo at the Chance Theater in Poughkeepsie, New York. The Chance is historically known for having an outstanding reputation, hosting many electrifying bands and well-known singers over the years. The owners are my good friends, Frank Pallett and his sister, Carolyn Pallett Brophy. This event is always exciting and fun. Band members carried in enormous pieces of equipment as I weaved in between others, who were a mixture of employees and attendees. Many there had more than half of their body tattooed. This is an annual event. I found my way to a dark corner, settled in, and waited. There is always a period of time before events actually start to take form, and this is my favorite time. There is a sense of excitement and stillness among the chaos. Scanning the faces of so many strangers and meeting their smiles with mine made the trip worthwhile.

Ever since I was a teenager, I had found my peace in the middle of music. As a pre-teen, I absorbed my body and soul into the complete collection of Simon and Garfunkel. Their lyrics found a strange home in my heart. My mind wandered far away from the difficult house I called my home. When I was a teenager, my mother's addiction to alcohol had grown into something unrealistic and bizarre to a youngster. My mother had a heart of gold, a true sense of humor, and a fine intellect. She had many highlights in her life; however, she lost her long battle with alcoholism. On her long road to recovery, she endured two stays in an inpatient rehabilitation center in High Watch, Connecticut. During her stay, I sent her many letters of support, including the words from the song "Mrs. Robinson."

In one letter, I explained how I felt at thirteen years old and how I felt Paul Simon was singing about a secret, such as alcoholism. Apparently, my mother, who agreed with my concept and suggestion in the lyrics, wrote me in return that she ecstatically showed her therapist my letter. I felt a personal victory in my effort to express my love to her, and I whispered "thank you" to the image on my Simon and Garfunkel album. This would be my only victory with my mother. As many people know, children of alcoholics often share the same mixed emotions and face many of the same uphill battles in silence. Later in life, I realized I strengthened my intuitive abilities unconsciously during the hardest years of her drinking. I often focused on the events that lay ahead and anticipated things prior to their happening. In 1985, sometime close to Easter, my mother left this world and entered the afterlife suddenly. Since then, I have embraced topics such as death, disease, addiction, and life through eyes I could now call "experienced."

I have found the need to continue to have empathy for those who have found themselves on the road to recovery. I have befriended musicians and twins Marc Kancler, whose legal name is Rock Star, and Kris Kancler, whose legal name is Super Star. I have supported their project, Rock Star Super Star (RSSS) and truly believe in their cause. Through music, Rock Star and Super Star have taken the opportunity to help young people understand addiction and educate them on prevention. I proudly have one of their videos embedded on my website, since I feel their music and efforts are amazing. Listening to the words of "Serenity" underscores the dedication, determination, and love these men have for each other and for others. It is truly a pleasure to know them.

My work as a psychic medium is important, but what is really important is that we, as psychics and mediums, have the sense of unity in any tragedy and focus using our gifts and abilities along with the power of prayer to be helpful. From my own experience with sudden death, there is nothing more painful than someone trying to minimize, eliminate, or act disrespectful in your time of devastating grief.

I have made it a point to ask those who have lost a loved one recently to take time in seeking out a mediumship reading. Grieving is difficult, and sometimes there is no time limit on how you should feel. Especially those who have experienced a sudden death need to take time to process the death, experience grieving, and absorb the shock they are feeling. I truly believe that neither I nor any medium can demand a spirit to show up in a reading. I believe the spirit steps forward with a message, and we cannot order one up, as I feel this would be unfair. I have been the medium, as well as been the sitter for some amazing, loving mediumship readings. It is very often the strangest details that arise in a reading that very often shows the spirit's personality, humor, and creativity. Very often, we get to see our loved ones in a dream, sometimes in the simple passing image of a person.

Recently, I saw a young man who resembled my ex-boyfriend, Glenn McLarnon, who died suddenly a few years ago. He was standing on the number 6 subway on the commute home. When I looked up, I saw his exact expression in the smile of a stranger. When the man turned and looked in my direction, he no longer looked like Glenn. But for that one instant, his smile and the squinting of his eyes were Glenn—no doubt in my mind. Glenn loved music and played guitar. Since he worked for Sam Ash Music Stores, he once took me as a guest to the Electric Lady Studios, in the early 1990s. The recording studio was originally built by Jimi Hendrix in 1970 and the studio designer was John

Storyk. The place was absolutely amazing as it was designed with lively, colorful, creative art murals. The Halloween party we attended there was unforgettable, as we both felt completely transcended into the 1960s. Glenn was always so much fun. I used to ask him to play Eric Clapton for me on his acoustic guitar. It was very heartwarming, since Glenn touched many people's lives and most likely left this world not knowing the great impact he truly made.

Many people gather at psychic events to share, discover, and create new connections. As a professional psychic medium, I have had some interesting questions from clients and curious people. Some questions include:

- Are you for real?
- Why do you wear black?
- Are you single?
- Can you see ghosts?
- Should I be afraid of you?

Some of the other questions I also hear are:

- Is my loved one still in pain?
- Is my animal in heaven?
- How long does it take to get to heaven?
- Can they still see us?

The second set of questions shows the honest curiosity that people have on their journey in life, as they somehow prepare for what lies in the unknown.

At this event at the Chance Theater, I was so interested in hearing the bands and seeing how the tattoo artists set up their work stations that I could have almost forgotten why I was there. Shortly after taking my tour, I was enchanted by a wonderful group of people, and before I knew it, the night was over. I had many people asking me about my readings and even asking me to explain some tattoos, using my work with symbols.

That night, I hoped I had helped all of the people I met, including the skeptics who were willing to "try out the psychic." I work within the white light, and some people ask, what is that? The white light, as I describe it, is protection, positive energy, coming from a truthful place of love and from God. I believe my information comes from the spirit world. I do not predict death of any kind. This is not my job. God is the only one, I believe, who calls us home. I have been very helpful with clients who are becoming ill, during their treatment, and in the process of prevention of disease. I am a healer, and I instruct others to heal themselves.

Driving home, I saw the moon through the windshield, guiding me on my long journey home. The night was like the entire day, a wonderful, exciting, musical, creative experience. Musical events are always energetic and electric. I remember attending the Woodstock Festival in 1994 and realizing how music touches generations of people and changes throughout history. Music has helped me in and out of troubled times and was always there somewhere in the distance, comforting me through some crazy, wonderful, and horrible experiences.

Throughout my life, music has become my friend, and many who play professionally have become my best friends. My very close friend Rob Caggiano from the bands Anthrax and The Damned Things, has taught me many things, but most important, he has taught me friendship. Rob was one of the first people in my life to believe in my psychic ability and encourage me to follow my heart and give readings. Rob has stayed in touch with me over his busy tour schedule and amazing music career, often informing me about new music, artists, bands, and even New Age stuff that I need to check out. I thank him every day for showing me things about life and the world that I would have never found without him. But most important, I thank him for helping me find the one thing I never thought I would, and that is myself.

I believe in the power of the moon, and I always have. As a little girl, I grew up in a house that had a mimosa tree whose branches touched my window. Mimosa has the loveliest scent and the prettiest pink flowers. I truly believe the mimosa was my introduction to my fascination and my love of the South. The tree felt tropical and expressed a feeling of escape for me. My young mind believed the moon sat behind the mimosa, peeking its way through for me to see.

Even as a small child, I made intentions on the moon and realized how the moon was symbolic of emotions and affected the sea and ocean. Making a moon intention is similar to making a wish, like blowing out candles on a birthday cake. Making an intention is a conscious and visual process. But the intention has to invoke creating something positive in your life or in others. Perhaps you desire to have a change in your life, such as a new job, home, or love. I have made many intentions on the moon for many clients, family, and friends. One favorite story I have is about a friend who was requesting a moon intention for a promotion in his police work. He asked me what he needed to do, and I said, "Nothing, just keep positive thoughts of your wishes for two or three full moons." I made the intention. My intentions to the moon are simple and consist of a combination of a dance and a chant. I always say, you have to believe, and when you do, anything is possible.

As I explain to my students, some things in life are not in our control. Many times, life teaches us lessons, and sometimes others learn from our lessons. This gives us experiences that help us grow and learn as we endure. Life is not fair, and if you look hard enough, it takes its turn with everyone, so sit back and watch. Not everyone has your life; some have it better or worse, but what you need to do is cherish yours. Like caring for a garden, nurture, care, and protect your life on its journey. We live one life, perhaps more, but the one we are living is happening right now, so don't let it speed by. All you have to do is grab it, acknowledge it, change it, love it, and most importantly, live it!

In 1989, I decided to get a tattoo. Many of my friends are owners and collectors of Harley-Davidson motorcycles, and I learned a lot about tattoos from them. Symbolism is huge for bikers and for me. It's especially meaningful for me, since I work closely with symbols in my psychic, coffee, and dream work. My tattoo had to tell a story with significance that would truly reflect my emotions. So I traveled to Big Joe Tattoo in Mount Vernon, New York, and received a tattoo from Big Joe Kaplan, the owner, who is now deceased. Joe was a big, friendly guy who was very nice and very patient with me.

I explained that I wanted a winged heart tattoo. I went through a detailed explanation of how I wanted wings that that would hold a suspended broken heart and have an almost invisible teardrop. Not long after my too-lengthy description, Joe had found the right stencil for me. He explained that he would not outline the heart in black, since he was convinced my heart would not always be broken and I would return to have it filled in. I knew I would never return. The wings meant my broken heart would always be free and no one would ever see the impact of the sadness it has caused, unless I let them get close enough to see the almost invisible teardrop.

The broken heart was not caused by one particular love but instead would symbolize several events in my life that did or will cause pain and heartbreak. This concept seems dark and mysterious to some, but like any tattoo, you have it for life, and this was mine. I have never wanted another tattoo and have no regrets about getting this one. Every picture has a story, like every person and every tattoo. The ink is faded today, and Joe is long gone, but my memories of both are still very bright. I am saying thank you to all of the tattoo artists, especially those who help define someone's life or help identify someone in their sudden death.

Chapter 11

Grand Central Station

In December 2011, I asked someone to meet me in Grand Central Station after work. The person was familiar with New York City, but I was unsure how familiar he was with Grand Central Station. I found choosing that place to meet would be symbolic for many reasons. I chose to meet him under the huge American flag that was hung just days after the September 11 attacks on the World Trade Center. He works in construction and had mentioned that he knew many men who lost their lives that day. I had served in Baghdad, Iraq, as an Army Reservist. The flag is a powerful symbol to many people but especially powerful after this tragic event in New York City. Every day of the year, that flag hangs there, and every day and night, American soldiers stand guard. Very often, you even see police officers with a guard dog. This is a constant reminder that the life we once knew has changed but who we are has not. Deep down inside, we understand, appreciate, and cherish those who made the ultimate sacrifice for our daily freedom.

Grand Central Station is the concept I have used to help form and name my company, Dream Central Station, LLC. As a little girl, my father worked at *Reader's Digest* magazine, which was in the Pan Am Building, inside Grand Central Station. On a few occasions, my father took me to work with him. One of my early memories is of him taking my hand and leading me across the main concourse to the escalator. At the end of the day, I couldn't wait to come back to the escalator and see the big green ceiling filled with stars. In 1998, the main concourse's ceiling renovation was completed. The long, vigorous renovation was done to remove the years of the environmental elements. Many passersby do not know two important facts about the ceiling. If you look up, you will notice that the sky is painted backward and the stars have been somewhat shifted out of place. There are many thoughts on this depiction of the sky; however, it is known that the Vanderbilt family felt this was God's view of the sky, and I tend to agree with that. It was there that I truly fell in love with art and the concept of being free. At five years old, I knew I would enjoy that ceiling for the rest of my life.

Grand Central Terminal is historic for many reasons. It was built in 1871 and is located at Forty-Second Street and Park Avenue in Midtown Manhattan. It is properly called Grand Central Terminal but often referred to as "Grand Central Station" by New Yorkers like me. It was rebuilt several times, with the most recent work completed in 2000. It was and is currently is a hub of transportation for millions of commuters and tourists every year. Grand Central, over the years, has housed countless shops and eateries. Many of my favorites are still there, such as the Oyster Bar and the bakery, known as Zaro's Bread Basket, as well as the brand-new Apple store, which opened just recently. Grand Central Station is a place where a traveler goes to get to another place, much the same as a person coming to me for insight and enlightenment to reach a better understanding or place in their lives through a psychic reading. Grand Central Station has three major railroad lines. Dream Central Station has many types of readings: coffee, automatic writing, photo reading, mediumship, and tarot cards.

That early December day, I met my friend under the American flag. I began our visit by leading a personal tour of the terminal. I took him across the main concourse and to the lower level, to the Magnolia Bakery to watch the staff members frost the delicious cupcakes. This level also has many of the same items as the one above, such as a florist stand where beautiful, delicate, sweet-smelling flowers can be purchased just prior to your train's departure. I showed him the fruit stand where you can get a fruit smoothie in no time flat. This level is where you can enter the Oyster Bar, a restaurant with a ton of fish items to choose from. I informed him that I took my very good friend Marilyn Whall, who is an Australian psychic medium, there for dinner this past summer. The symbolism of fish varies for many people, but I have always found it to be a sign of good financial fortune.

When we returned to the main concourse, I decided to take him up and down the escalator, telling him about the ceiling and the significance it has had on me for so many years. Grand Central practically sparkled that evening. Perhaps it was because it was nearing Christmastime, and the place was filled with colorful decorations and pumped with high energy. However, I tend to believe that the symbolism of our meeting was strangely individually important. I was able to see this place that I have seen a thousand times for the first time through someone else's eyes. Many times in life, we need to step away from ourselves, and as odd as it sounds, step into someone else, in order to see the world slightly differently. Seeing the world differently can truly help us to understand and appreciate it all the better.

That evening, as we stopped on the stairs to reflect on the massive crowds that filled the terminal, we witnessed various different scenes: a man playing music for spare change, a couple kissing good-bye, a policeman waking up a homeless person, a shopkeeper packing up. In the distance, someone was watching us watching them, and this why there is no place like Grand Central Station—one of the only places you can be invisible and noticed at the same time. The various scenes we saw that night are now glimpses and memories to me. But it's important to remember that we aren't always able to know everything that will become our future. By searching through the unknown, you may be more than surprised to find what you will soon discover to be your "new" future.

ABOUT THE AUTHOR

Catherine Nadal's gifts of spirit communication have been with her since she was nine years old. As a child, she realized she was able to see, hear, and communicate with spirit guides through dreams and during waking hours. Her special natural gifts have given her the ability to help others through grief, crisis, stress, and joyful moments in their lives. She has a true belief in the afterlife and has helped many others find their spiritual path.

Catherine is a psychic, medium, and clairvoyant. She is an active member of the Eyes of Learning in Long Island. She has trained at the Arthur Findlay School in Stansted, England, and also has studied with Suzane Northrop and James Van Praagh in psychic workshops at Omega Institute. For the past seven years, she has worked numerous public events, which include psychic fairs, teachings, and live demonstrations in the New York City and New Jersey area. She believes in working within the white light and is very prayerful. She also leads guided meditations, which helps students utilize their gifts and develop their hidden psychic abilities. She has international and well-known clients in the music and entertainment business. Catherine has been a guest on radio shows such as *The Malice Cooper Radio Show* and *Getting on Top with Paul Morris*, sharing her psychic skills and unique readings. Tina Wilson from *Global Entertainment* magazine hosted a radio interview with Catherine as her psychic medium guest.

Recently, Catherine has been involved with paranormal investigations of historical buildings, which includes the Chance Theater in Poughkeepsie and the Iron Island Museum in Buffalo, New York. Catherine has participated during the month of October for Halloween, as a psychic medium at the Festival of the Dead—the Annual Psychic Fair and Witchcraft Expo in Salem, Massachusetts.

Catherine believes that life is a journey. After serving a one-year tour in Iraq with the military, Catherine realized life is short, and she needed to work more with the public in assisting them on their spiritual journey. Her knowledge of the spirit world has motivated her to help others better understand, evaluate, and review relationships and love. She believes that even through dying, our loved ones never say good-bye, even when it feels like they have left us behind. She knows and trusts that our loved ones are helping to guide and protect us.

Led by spirit, Catherine has read Italian and Turkish coffee since her late teens. Through working with coffee, she has been able to help her clients identify issues in their lives and find solutions. She delivers unusual coffee readings, which leave lasting impressions with her clients.

Catherine works with children in teaching them about the phases of the moon. She gives instructions on moon dancing and intentions to both children and adults. She enjoys working with children to help them understand their psychic abilities and seeing spirits.

Today, she runs Dream Central Station; as a light worker, Catherine is able to assist others to discover and explore their spiritual journey. The concept behind Dream Central Station was developed with the famous Grand Central Station in New York City in mind. This station is a location and landmark that assists people in getting to different locations and destinations in life. The station is busy, like the world we live in, which helps us complete our journey and experience. She believes that you need to continually grow, expand, and develop to better experience all of the divine gifts of life and the spirit world.